TAORMINA

.....PEARL OF THE MEDITERRANEAN.....

Publisher: F.lli MISTRETTA s.r.l.
Via Colonnello Missori, 18 PALERMO, Italy
Tel. 47.48.95

ILLUSTRATIONS

In the same series

SICILY
THE ISLAND IN THE SUN **pages 166**

PIAZZA ARMERINA
THE IMPERIAL VILLA OF CASALE **» 64**

Design, photography, lay out, and text by Lanfranco Angeli.

Published by: F.lli Mistretta, Editori in Palermo (Italy).
Printed by: Fotometalgrafica Emiliana, San Lazzaro di Savena, Bologna (Italy), July 1990

(The 1635 Baroque fountain. The sculpted figure of the female centaur, the city's emblem, is borne atop the two, tiered cups).

INTRODUCTION

Lying along the southernmost slopes of the Peloritani mountains, at 250 metres up on the rocky plateau of Mount Tauro, a sheer cliff rising from the Ionian Sea, is Taormina. The enchanting splendours of its natural landscape beckon travellers from all over the world. Set between the azure-tinted sky round the volcanic Mt Aetna – now fire-thrusting in eruption, now placid snow-mantled peak in dormancy – and the Ionian beaches, it enjoys a mild maritime climate which keeps its luxuriant gardens in flower the year round and makes it an unrivalled host for winter holidays.
The mountains descending towards Capo Sant'Andrea and the picturesque beaches of Mazzarò and Isola Bella are a triumph of colour with their palm trees, gardens of oranges and lemons and lush flora of subtropical plants. And the mythical Ionian coastline which extends outwards at the feet of Taormina has been celebrated in song and story since the most remote of ancient times.
Homer makes it the setting of legendary events – the discovery of the Island by the god Poseidon (Neptune) who makes it a gift to his sons, the Cyclopes, the home of Titans, Lotus Eaters and Laestrygonians, the site of the battle between Odysseus and the Cyclops, Polyphemus, who is blinded by the wily hero as he and his men make their escape from the monster's fiendish designs. Even the very place names of the area are a living reminder of these tales – Aci Trezza, Aci Castello, the Riviera dei Ciclopi. History, too, is present. At the foot of Mount Tauro, on the plateau which is today the site of Giardini, Greeks from Chalcis founded, after establishing the settlement of Cuma in the Gulf of Naples, their first colony in Sicily at the mouth of the Akesines (today Alcantara) river – Naxos. The magnificent cultural, historical and artistic heritage of the city, its mild climate and its incomparable natural beauty have been a magnet for travellers since the mideighteent century.

In the early years of this century, prior to the outbreak of World War I, Taormina played host to the wealthy and powerful: the Rothschilds, Morgans, Krupps, Edward the VII and George V of England, Kaiser Wilhelm II of Germany, and the Kings of Siam and Tonkin, and the writers Anatole France and Gabriele d'Annunzio, who were followed in more recent times by the French writer, Roger Peyrefitte. The Russian prince, Yusupof, one of Rasputin's assassins, also stayed here briefly.
Others, notably the English and Germans, even established more permanent residence in Taormina, either acquiring property or having villas built. Otto Geleng, the painter, Karl Stempel, a Lett, Wilhelm Von Gloeden, the famous German aesthete and photographer, and D.H. Lawrence, the renowned English novelist and poet, were among their number. And, although many could not lay claim to noble lineage, they were, in the words of Pietro Nicolosi, whose scholarly book chronicles the life of the city, the «Barons of Taormina».
These illustrious personages were the first to discover the uniqueness of the city and sound the clarion. Nor did their call go unheeded. Financiers, captains of industry and many leading members of Europe's aristocracy were captivated by its charms and made it their winter resort for many years. Particular mention in this respect is due Baron Wilhelm Von Gloeden, through whose efforts the splendours and beauty of Taormina were revealed to the entire world. Born on the 16th of September 1856 in the family castle of Volkashagen near Wismar, Germany, the young baron went to Taormina at the insistence of his friend, Otto Geleng, who had then been living in the city for some time in the hope that the mild climate might alleviate, if not cure, his consumption (tuberculosis).
Although Von Gloeden initially enjoyed the carefree existence that wealth and social status entitled him to, the family fortunes suffered a severe reverse several years thereafter and the young nobleman found himself more an heir of penury than vast estates. Abandoned by many of his former friends, Von Gloeden was saved from total indigence by the small gratuities he received from time to time by the Duke of Mecklemburg, to whom Von Gloeden had often sung the praises of Taormina in letters and picture postcards. The baron's descriptions and accompanying illustrations intrigued and attracted the duke, who later sent Von Gloeden a large, 30x40 cm camera – as much to help his needy friend as to encourage him to make a photographic record of the natural beauties of this Sicilian garden.
Necessity is the mother of invention, and never has such an adage proved more prophetic than in the case of Von Gloeden. He quickly mastered the techniques of his medium and, guided by his personal aesthetic canon as much as by his proclivities, set out to exalt the beauty of the male figure in his art. He would photograph young adolescent boys from the area in nude or scantily clad poses set in the bucolic, pastoral world of Taormina's countryside and coast. The themes of these compositions were culled from Greek classicism and its mythological figures, which were infused with a new life by the magic of the photographer. The baron-cum-photographic artist could not have chosen a more ideal locale for his strikingly beautiful images than Taormina – a site so imbued by the deeds and songs of the Homeric tradition.
Von Gloeden's art was an immediate and enthusiastic success, occasioned equally by the originality of the genre and its thematic material, both of which were subjected to the passion and sensitivity of the aesthete. After centuries of neglect and oblivion, Taormina was rediscovered through the art of Wilhelm Von Gloeden and became for both decadent social dandy no less than the fortunate traveller of the day an experience not to be missed.
Today, as a living testimonial to the baron-photographer and his creative genius, private concerns, public agencies and associations are dedicating numerous publications honouring his work. For such celebrations are only fitting to Taormina, itself acclaimed the world over as a foremost resort. Luxury hotels and intimate traditional pensions cater to every taste and need of the modern traveller, even in expanding their services in conjunction with the city's tourism expansion to include Naxos, Schisò, Giardini, Letoianni and Capo Sant'Alessio.
Taormina is the point of departure for an almost endless number of excursions, each of which bears eloquent testimony to the millennia of Sicilian history. Aetna, the Gole of Alcantara, the ancient and stately Randazzo, the Riviera of the Ciclopi (Acicastello and Acitrezza, the settings of the novels, *I Malavoglia* and *Mastro Don Gesualdo*, by the famous Sicilian writer, Giovanni Verga), and, farther on towards Catania, the Roman Piazza Armerina, to name but a few.
The best way for the newly arrived traveller to get acquainted with Taormina is a walking tour of the city itself. This offers the tourist the perfect opportunity to take in the many distinctive sights and sounds of Taormina, to acquire a feeling of the city as one explores the picturesque streets with their craft and antiques shops – which often have veritable works of art within for the discerning eye – and buildings, the balconies of which are bedecked with flowers.
This setting is dominated by the Graeco-roman amphitheatre, the second largest of its kind still extant, which is unique per se and for the spectacular view it affords from its heights of the Ionian Sea, the Calabrian coast and the smoke-plumed Mt Aetna. Even the seasoned traveller cannot but admire the splendours which lie everywhere about – the polychromed Palazzo Corvaia of the Quattrocento (1400s), seat of the first Sicilian Parliament, the Romanesque-gothic churches, the Palazzo of the Duchi di Santo Stefano (Dukes of St Stephen), the Roman remains of the Naumachie (sea battles) and Odeon Theatre, the church of Santa Maria del Piliere with its magnificent portal and rose window, the Aragonese Palazzo Ciampoli, the Badia Vecchia (Old Abbey), the Duomo of San Nicola (1300s) with its imposing square plan and sharp crenellations, and San Domenico, a historic monastery which is now a luxury hotel.
Yet as noted previously, it is the narrow streets and lanes of the city's centre which will reveal to and reward the discerning gaze with unexpected pleasures. Here, in the simple and unassuming façades, can be seen Roman epigraphs, sculpted medallions of ancient dwellings, Greek columns and capitals incorporated in the façades of the buildings, themselves a harmonious array of alternating styles and epochs – Moorish, Romanesque, Gothic and Aragonese. And, as befits the personality and mood of such a unique city, visitors are invited to relax and refresh themselves in the central Piazza 9 Aprile, the

so-called «sitting-room» of Taormina, with its many fine caffés and spacious terrace, which offers an enchanting panorama of Aetna and the Bay of Giardini. Taormina is all this and much more for, together with the warmth and aristocratic hospitality of its people, it has cast its spell on visitors from every corner of the globe.

TAORMINA: A BRIEF HISTORY

Despite the numerous palaeolithic artifacts which have been brought to light, nothing can be stated with any certainty about the original inhabitants of Sicily save that the island was settled from the earliest prehistory. The dawn of the Neolithic brought the migrations of new peoples who introduced the potter's art. The archaeological record clearly shows the evolution of these artifacts from primitive, sun-dried pieces to more sophisticated, fired pottery of increasingly complex decorative motifs.

Towards the end-phase of the Neolithic, subsequent migrations brought the Sicanians, Siculans and the Elimi (of Mediterranean, probably Mesopotamian, origin), whom we shall come upon again with the rise of history.

The strategic heights upon which Taormina stands today were occupied in *ca.* 13th-12th century B.C. by the Siculans. Distinct from the Sicanians, the Siculans are thought to be of Thracian-Illyrian-Cretan origin and related to the Siculoti people of Dalmatia (from R. von Scala). The first artifacts connected with the original people of the zone were initially brought to light in the area round Cocolonazzo, along the road to Mola at the foot of the rocky cliff upon which is situated the town of Castel Mola. Beneath the overlying strata of Graeco-roman ruins are a necropolis and other remains which bear eloquent witness to a now silent Siculan settlement.

The Siculan city of Tauromenion was soon to establish contact with Greek civilization. In all probability, the Chalcidic colonists who had founded the city of Naxos at the foot of Mt Tauro along the coast sent several contingents of settlers to secure the Siculan heights. With the destruction of Naxos in 392 B.C. by Dionysius of Syracuse, the surviving colonists were allowed to settle in Tauromenion in 358 B.C., through the intervention of Andromach, the father of the historian, Timeus, and establish a Greek city. Andromach was the leading statesman and military strategist of Taormina at the time. An able administrator and tactician, he reformed the city government, introduced a constitution guaranteeing the election of public officials and successfully repelled Carthaginian attempts to conquer the area.

Taormina thereafter enters a period in which its history is inextricably bound up with the fortunes of Syracuse. After being conquered by Agathocles, it falls first under the rule of Carthage and subsequently under that of the tyrant, Tindarion, an ally of Pyrrhus, king of Epirus, whose policies gave rise to a renewed flowering of Sicily after the latter had successfully protected Syracuse against Carthaginian attack. Taormina later became part of the kingdom of Geron II and, upon his death, was conquered together with the rest of the island by the power of Rome.

During the Second Punic War (211 B.C.), Tauromenium was a staunch ally of Rome and, because of its loyalty, granted annexation to the provincial territories and the special status and privileges of a «civitas foederatae» or city of the federation, a designation which was enjoyed by only two other cities in Roman Sicily – Messana and Neeto (five other cities, Panormo, Alesa, Centuripe, Alicie and Segesta were exempt only from the «decima», the tithe or tenth-part tax, without being granted full status).

Slavery was introduced in the wake of the Second Punic War and brought about the conditions which spawned the ensuing Slave Wars. Taorminium became a rebel stronghold during the insurrections and had to be conquered by the consul, Rupilius, who finally crushed the uprising. Later still it would be the scene of a military setback for Octavian (Augustus) in his struggle for power against S. Pompey (34 B.C.). In fact the future emperor was thereafter to establish a military garrison in the city because of its strategic importance.

Roman dominion provided the impetus for agricultural development and Sicily became the granary of Rome. Julius Caesar, and Antony after him, bestowed Roman citizenship and law upon the island's inhabitants, although this established order was quite effectively undermined by the brief but thoroughly oppressive policies of the propraetor, Verrus.

Roman rule also meant economic prosperity and Sicily too became the site of monumental public works and buildings. The Greek amphitheatres were restored and expanded while new theatres were erected to accommodate the scale of Roman spectacles.

Aqueducts, military and commercial ports to handle the increasing trade with both east and west, and, of course, a network of roads girding the island's coastal perimeter (with inland links between Syracuse and Catania in the direction of Agrigento and Palermo) were laid out and constructed.

Taormina also benefited from this feverish display of public largesse. The Greek amphitheatre was renovated and enlarged, aqueducts built and sewers installed. The Odeon, a second smaller theatre, was subsequently erected, and, perhaps even more significant, a great many Romans began to build their villas here. Attracted by the healthy climate and the scenic beauty of the area, the Romans became in fact tourists *ante litteram* – a point emphatically underscored by the recent discovery on the outskirts of the city of decorative flooring mosaics which had once belonged to these villas.

Following the fall of the Roman Empire, Taormina became the capital of Byzantine power in Sicily (9th century A.D.) by virtue of its position, fortifications, cultural heritage and urban development. With the invasion of the island at Mazara in June of 827, the forces of Islam began their conquest. The seige of Taormina was undertaken in 902 by Ibn Ahmed and, although the beleaguered city withstood fierce assaults for decades, it finally fell to the Arabs in 962 and was completely destroyed. The caliph, Al Muezz, renamed the city «Almoezia» and within a few short years had it rebuilt, its beauty now surpassing even its former splendour. The Normans invade the island shortly thereafter, putting an end to Moslem domination. Following a siege of several months, Taormina yields to Roger of Altavilla in 1079.

The subsequent history of the city is a chronicle of the shifting politico-military alliances which thenceforth dominate the larger pattern of European history. During the war of the Sicilian Vespers (1282), Taormina remains faithful to the Aragonese of Spain; and in 1410 the first Sicilian Parliament is convened here at the Palazzo Corvaia to elect Frederick, Count of Luna, King of Sicily. The city was repeatedly used as the currency of barter by the kings of Spain; yet despite such regal insouciance, its loyalty never swerved – not even when the city of Messina rebelled in 1675 and Taormina was briefly occupied by the French troops of Louis XIV. Shortly thereafter the Spanish troops of Philip V, despite opposition from the soldiers of Filangieri (whose patriotism is rewarded when he is made Duke of Taormina), regain possession of the city.

As Spanish power in the Mediterranean declines in the ensuing years, the historical importance and place in European affairs of Sicily ebbs just as inexorably. It thenceforth merely reflects the light of the major powers, but no longer radiates any of its own. At first bartered away in the political intrigues of England, Austria and France, it becomes part of the kingdom of Savoy when the Sicilian crown is given to Vittorio Amedeo of Savoy by the Treaty of Utrecht (Sicily fought against the Franco-spanish troops).

In 1718 following their acquisition of Gibraltar and Majorca, England vies with France for dominance in the Mediterranean. Sicily is ceded to Austria in exchange for Sardinia after the wars of the Grand Alliance. In 1734 during the war of succession to the Polish throne, Charles of Bourbon, moving rapidly to preclude English intervention, unseats the Austrians and claims possession of Naples and Sicily. He is crowned King of Naples and Sicily one year later on July 3rd 1735 during solemn investiture ceremonies in the Duomo of Palermo.

During the years preceding 1848 (the year marking the revolt of Sicily against the Bourbons), Taormina languished without distinction in the general decline of the island itself. This state of affairs was abruptly reversed when, on April the 9th, 1860, the city courageously fought for its freedom from the Bourbon yoke during the struggles of Sicilian liberation. Although defeated, the city was finally to gain its freedom with the arrival of Garibaldi's troops, whose efforts were to lead to the reunification of Sicily to Italy.

(Photo by Nino Malambri)

THE LIDO OF MAZZARÒ

An alluring beach protected by rocks, a snug bay framed by flowers and the lush vegetation of palms, citrus and banana trees, Here is the sea, its shimmering essence, its taste and touch are immediate, alive—even on a crowded day. Here, detached from everyday cares, the pace of life slows, an air of tranquil serenity sets in and the hours of the day soften in the rhytmic, entrancing colours of the surrounding nature. The sea is limpid, its colours shining—now green, now azure almost indistinguishable from the sky, then deep blue as the wind-swept swells are hurled billowing upon the rocks. The «placid Ionian» is a calm sea throughout much of the year, even in winter; its glimmer a reminder of the Homeric legends of yore, its serenity the silent spell of the sleepy elements.
Above, on the hills which gradually slope towards the sandy shore, is the town. Set among the olive groves and surrounded by the ever blooming vegetation, visitors will find the hotels, small pensions and the Grand Hotel Mazzarò, a stately haven of elegant hospitality. At the northern end of the beach, there is a fishing village nestled within the semicircle of a small landing. The small boats are made by craftsmen from the oak in the woods about Aetna, and, outfitted with the picturesque «lampare» (lantern) for night fishing, are the mainstay of the fishing fleet whose fresh catch is supplied to restaurants or sold by itinerant fishmongers in the town's streets. During the peak season, the fishermen become tourist guides and ferry visitors who wish to discover the other beautiful beaches along the coast—the Baia delle Sirene (Sirens' Bay), the rocky cliffs of Capo Sant'Andrea (St Andrew's Cape), the sheer crags of Capo Taormina and its offshore, upjutting rock formations, and the sandy cove from which the beautiful and solitary Isola Bella emerges and the entrance to the Grotta Azzurra is found. A cable-car service connecting Taormina to the Lido of Mazzarò and the surrounding beaches shuttles visitors in but a few minutes from the hotels above to the coast below. A more scenic route is the coast road (Statale 114) to the city. Its serpentine path meanders among the villas of Taormina and their luxuriant gardens, and each curve reveals spectacular panoramas which will long remain vivid in the mind's eye—the snow-capped, smoke-plumed spectacle of Aetna and the azure mirror of the Ionian Sea outlined against the rocky spurs of the Aspromonte.

The Mazzarò Sea Palace beach. Foreground: The seamen's boats of the fishing village. Even in winter it is not unusual to see visitors from the more northerly climes of Europe swimming or sun-bathing on the beach, delighted at the mild Sicilian winter.

LA PIGNA CABINE AMERICAN BAR

The picturesque fishing village at Lido di Mazzarò. Well-ordered and inviting, it is the departure point for tours of the coast by boat. More often than not, just-caught fish can be purchased directly from the fishermen. As the village is closed to automobile traffic, it can only be reached on foot through a scenic lane bordered by private homes with their flower-decked balconies and splendid gardens.

View of Isola Bella from the 170-m high Guardiola Vecchia located at the base of the plateau upon which the Graeco-roman amphitheatre stands. It is encircled by prickly-pear trees, the symbol of the Sicilian landscape. The eternal and enrapturing spectacle of nature itself, undiminished in beauty, is another of the area's unforgettable sights.

A panoramic view of Lido di Mazzarò with its modern tourist and beach facilities, large hotels and intimate pensions, all set off against the spurs of the southern Nebrodi peaks with Mt Veneretta among them. Up on the hills, mid-way along the coast, are the newer districts of Taormina. On the top of the sheer cliff is the town of Castel Mola, a natural balcony which affords a panorama of rare and splendid beauty.

Preceding pages, large plate: Overall view of the Lido di Mazzarò. The tourist facilities which have helped spread the renown of Taormina's hospitality throughout the world can be seen on the ever verdant, sloping hills.

ISOLA BELLA (BELLE ISLE) - Isola Bella rises from the water in this sandy cove, its solitary beauty unspoiled by the several small hotels which are discretly set back from the beach. It is without doubt the most impressive and memorable of Taormina's beaches. The bright, clear sea, the resonant silence of the golden beaches, the rock formations wreathing the isle—glimmering under and reflecting the intense light of the warm Mediterranean sun—and set off by the vibrant azure of sea and sky offer the beholder an unforgettable view.
A short boat ride, though it would not be beyond the prowess of an experienced, strong swimmer, will take the visitor to the splendid marine grottoes of Capo Sant'Andrea, where a four-centimeter water line above the waves can be seen.

Or, by sailing southward, you come upon Capo Taormina and the giant rock formations thrusting up from the seabed. The abundance and variety of fish in these clear coastal waters make this an ideal spot for scuba fishing.

(Following pages, large plate: Isola Bella immersed in the calm and shimmering afternoon light).
ISOLA BELLA AND CAPO SANT'ANDREA - The splendour of this magnificent marine-scape is enhanced by the unspoiled natural beauty of the small bay. One's gaze can sweep unobstructed from the expanse of the Ionian Sea to the Calabrian coast and the first rugged spurs of the Aspromonte peaks.

ISOLA BELLA, in the opalescent dawn glow, immersed in the crystal transluscence of the Ionian Sea and tinged by the golden rays of the breaking sun. In this oasis set between the azure of sky and sea and protected by inaccessible sheer rock walls the silence is broken only by light lapping of the waves on the soft sand and the strident cry of the wheeling gulls.

A view of the offshore rock formations emerging from the sea near Capo Taormina. Nature offers the visitor a glimpse of the elemental force and intrinsic beauty of the transparent unspoiled sea in the architecture of the coastal rocks, carved by the incessant action of the waves.

The Grand Hotel Capo Taormina, one of the entire coast's most prestigious hotels, stands atop the sheer rock wall. A model of modern elegance, it enhances the city's renown as a resort and also provides an ideal setting for international events and conferences.

THE GROTTA AZZURRA - This is the largest of the marine grottoes set in the rocky cliffs of Capo Sant'Andrea. It is easily reached by a short boat ride and is accessible to rafts. The visitor is greeted by one of nature's wonders wherein is renewed the eternal magic of its touch. Created by the shimmering undulations of the waves, the reflections on the limestone walls resemble delicate lace while the bright and dancing colours recall a world of enchantment. And the water gently lapping against the rock resounds throughout the cave as if echoing the song of the sea.

16 The offshore rock formations, crenellated by the waves, provide scenic splendour at the base of Capo Taormina.

Above: The remains of the Moslem necropolis which is presumed to overlay that of the preceding Byzantine period. Dating to *ca*. 1000 A.D., it consists of loculi (burial niches) placed one atop the other.

CHIESA DEI S.S. PIETRO E PAOLO (The Church of Sts. Peter and Paul) - Believed to be the oldest Catholic church of Taormina, it was probably erected on the ruins of an ancient Greek temple and is said to be of Byzantine origin. That this view is consistent with the historical record can be deduced from the archaeological findings. These include a fine head of Zeus, brought to light by one of the dukes of St. Stephen, Biagio de Spuches, whose discoveries involve other artifacts as well, and the «Tavola dei Ginnasiarchi» (Tablet of the Gymnasiarchs, i.e. an epigraphical stele listing the names of the officials who were in charge of the gymnasium) unearthed by the Dutch archaeologist, Philippe d'Orville.

THE CAROUSEL TAORMINA - Crad

uments - Folk Traditions and Lore.

PALAZZO CIAMPOLI - Erected in 1412 as the crest above the stately entrance bears witness, this austere building stands at the head of a short stairway in the old city centre. It is a two-storey, Gothic-catalan style house with five, two-light mullioned windows on the façade and others, of more ornate motifs, on the side facing south. The Palazzo was originally embellished by an internal front courtyard which was entered through a door (photo, right) decorated by two sculpted medallions depicting ancient Romans.

Preceding pages, large plate: A capsule view of Taormina's landscape, monuments, nature and folklore. The brush-stroke images and scenes represent an overview which presupposes a more intimate acquaintance of the living essence of Taormina, a place one can come to love as well as admire.

Civilization - Millenary History - Eternal Natural Beauty - Famous Mo

◂ CHIESA DI SAN MICHELE ARCANGELO (Church of St Michael Archangel) - Probably erected in 1600, this Baroque church is distinguished by the subdued lines of the main portal and in its architrave and Ionic-inspired capitals, which recall the pediments of the Greek temples.

CHIESA AND CONVENTO DI SAN DOMENICO (Church and Monastery of St Dominic) - This building complex was originally founded by the nobleman and monk, Girolamo De Luna, in 1374. However it was the Prince of Cerami, Damiano Rosso degli Altavilla, a courtier and diplomat in the service of Alphonse V, King of Aragon and Sicily, who in becoming a monk first provided the monastery with a generous endowment and then, upon his death in 1430, bequeathed his entire estate, including the ancestral castle, so that church and monastery might find permanent appointment. One of the provisions in the Prince's will, however, stated that should the inheritance be used for purposes other than those intended by the donor (i.e. cease to house the monastery), then the entire estate would again become the possession of the noblemen's rightful heirs. Thus it was that in 1866, by enforcement of the Mancini Act which suppressed and expropriated the holdings of the religious orders, the Princes of Cerami once again regained their title to the monastery and subsequently transformed it into the most prestigious of Taormina's hotels.

At its founding in 1374, the church was named after and dedicated to St Agatha, virgin and martyr as well as the venerated patron saint of Catania, who suffered martyrdom by having her breasts cut off in the 4th century under the reign of Diocletian in the city of Taormina. After the bequest of the Prince of Cerami, the Dominican monks named the church St Mary of the Annunciation, the appellation it kept until its destruction in World War II. A statue of St Agatha is still to be seen in the Duomo of Taormina. It is the work of Martino Montanini and was sculpted for the church of the monastery in 1400.
From 1500 to 1640 this same church underwent substantial renovation and embellish-

ment, the work of expert local craftsmen. Their artistry and painstaking labour was mainly concentrated on the altars, which were adorned with mosaics and inlay work in polychrome marble from the Taormina quarries. The remains of the main altar are eloquent testimony to their art and dedication. Other notable features of the church were the magnificent carved-wood choir and sacristy wardrobes by the Dominican priest, Giuseppe Alermo, and the monumental *sacella* (chapels) of the city's nobles such as those of Giovanni Corvaia, Giuseppe Lombardo, jurist, and Ascanio Marziani, who established and financed the first hospital of Taormina (St Vincent's) in 1609.

(Photographs: Detail of the cloister with its splendid portals).
(The tabernacle used by the Dominican fathers to keep the holy oil for the sacrament of the last rites).

On July the 9th 1943, the blind fury of war completely devastated the church, leaving only the bell tower still intact. A conference hall was later built on the site in 1970 as part of the San Domenico Palace Hotel complex.
Largely untouched by the bombs of 1943, the monastery houses an inner cloister which dates from the 1500s. Its vaulted arcade is supported by single-stone columns with Ionic marble capitals. The central, Seicento (1600s) well is wreathed by splendid palms, magnolias, hybiscus and bougainvillaea, while the cloister walls bear ancient epigraphs, bas-reliefs of sarcophagi and magnificent portals from the 1500s. Of particular interest and mention is the large garden which surrounds the monastery. Perennially in flower, it is arranged in sloping terraces, a highly original and unique design which makes the garden a natural balcony on the scenic.

splendours of the Ionian Sea and Aetna.
Begging the indulgence of the reader, we should here like to quote the text of a bronze plaque which is located at the entrance to the garden. The anonymous author has dedicated it to an unknown English woman: «Her garden of remembrance: Here, in this sunlit garden, She rested under the protective shade of its trees. In this delightful garden so close to the Ionian Sea, She planted a tree in memory. For in this tranquil garden the flowers blossom and, in their blooming, each day recount a tale of love and, each hour of the silent night, in their fragrance, speak of Her who did love them so». There is no finer tribute, no word to add.

LA BADIA VECCHIA (The Old Abbey) - Also called «O Badiazza» in the dialect of Taormina, the name itself seems to have gained currency in the remote past when the building served to house a monastic order. In its plan, exterior architecture and other aspects, the Abbey is very similar to the Palazzo dei Duchi di Santo Stefano (Palace of the Dukes of St Stephen). Dating to the 14th century, it is a two-storey, rectangular plan building and is believed to have been part of a much larger edifice, of which it was the main fortified structure in the medieval city. In form and decorative design, this splendid historical monument bears witness to the so-called «chiaramontana» transition period, i.e. the use of oriental-inspired motifs (derived from the Normans) grafted on to the Gothic. At the end of the 1400s, the Catalan influences are then added to this style of architecture which wholly ignores the Renaissance forms and retains the

rich and inventive patterns of the Gothic. Characterized by the alternate play of tufa (porous stones) and lava stones, these ornamental motifs are a main feature of Norman architecture, notable examples of which are found everywhere in Sicily as well as in Taormina and nearby Randazzo.
The photograph shows details of the external stairway leading to the main entrance which is flanked by two different mullioned windows.

Left: a classic example of Gothic architecture with the pointed arch and finely ornamented rose window. Right: a «chiaramontana» style, mullioned window with rounded arch and transversal decoration of alternating tufa and lava stone wedges. The natural setting of the Abbey is also singular—high up the hill slopes overlooking the medieval district, a reminder, together with the austere battlements, that the Abbey also served as a fortress.

L'ISOLA BELLA E CAPO SANT'ANDREA

«To die is beautiful
In sight of the world's most beautiful sea!
Hand in Hand we walked out upon the rocks
Between Isola Bella and the Cape,
Happy as two lovers.
To die is beautiful
in sight of the world's most beautiful sea!»
(The sorrow and anguish in verse of two lovers, Frederick Naumann and Margaret Beyer, whose desperate flight from their own country was to end here in a tragedy of love. Was their sad end somehow mitigated by the overwhelming beauty of the locale? They indeed answer yes!)

VILLA COMUNALE (Commune Villa, Duke Colonna di Cesarò) - The Villa is a lush and flowering oasis, overflowing with plants of every kind. Here more than anywhere else one can pause and calmly contemplate the spectacular panorama—the sea by Giardini, Aetna, and the valley through which the Alcantara river meanders before silently coursing into the limpid waters of the Ionian. The master gardeners of the communal government go to great lengths in caring for this verdant splendour, a symbol of nature's generosity and of Taormina's most representative flora.

Photographs: Two views of the Villa: Snow-capped Aetna emerging from the tenuous haze of the valley below; and, one of the garden's lanes and year-round flowers crowned by the peak upon which stands the austere Castel Taormina.

THE GRECO-ROMAN THEATRE - The building of the hellenic theatre was probably begun in the 3rd century B.C.; under Gerone, The Romans, in the imperial period made important restorations and enlargements, thanks to the extension of the external walls and to the enlargement of the cavea. The orchestra floor is the same. Second to the Greek theatre of Syracuse for importance and dimension. The spectacle for the visitors is really beautiful: the theatre is situated behind volcano Etna and the blue sea. It is one of the most beautiful landscapes of the world because man succeeded in creating a beautiful jewel between the blue sky, and the blue sea, the green valley and the white tops of Etna. Its widest diameter is 109 m. and 35 m. is the orchestras' diameter. It was enlarged and almost entirely rebuilt in Roman times, perhaps in the 2nd century, in order to be utilized for gladiatorial spectacles. The capacity was of 5400 seats, with a perfect acoustic that still remains nowadays.

PLANIMETRY OF THE GREEK - ROMAN THEATRE

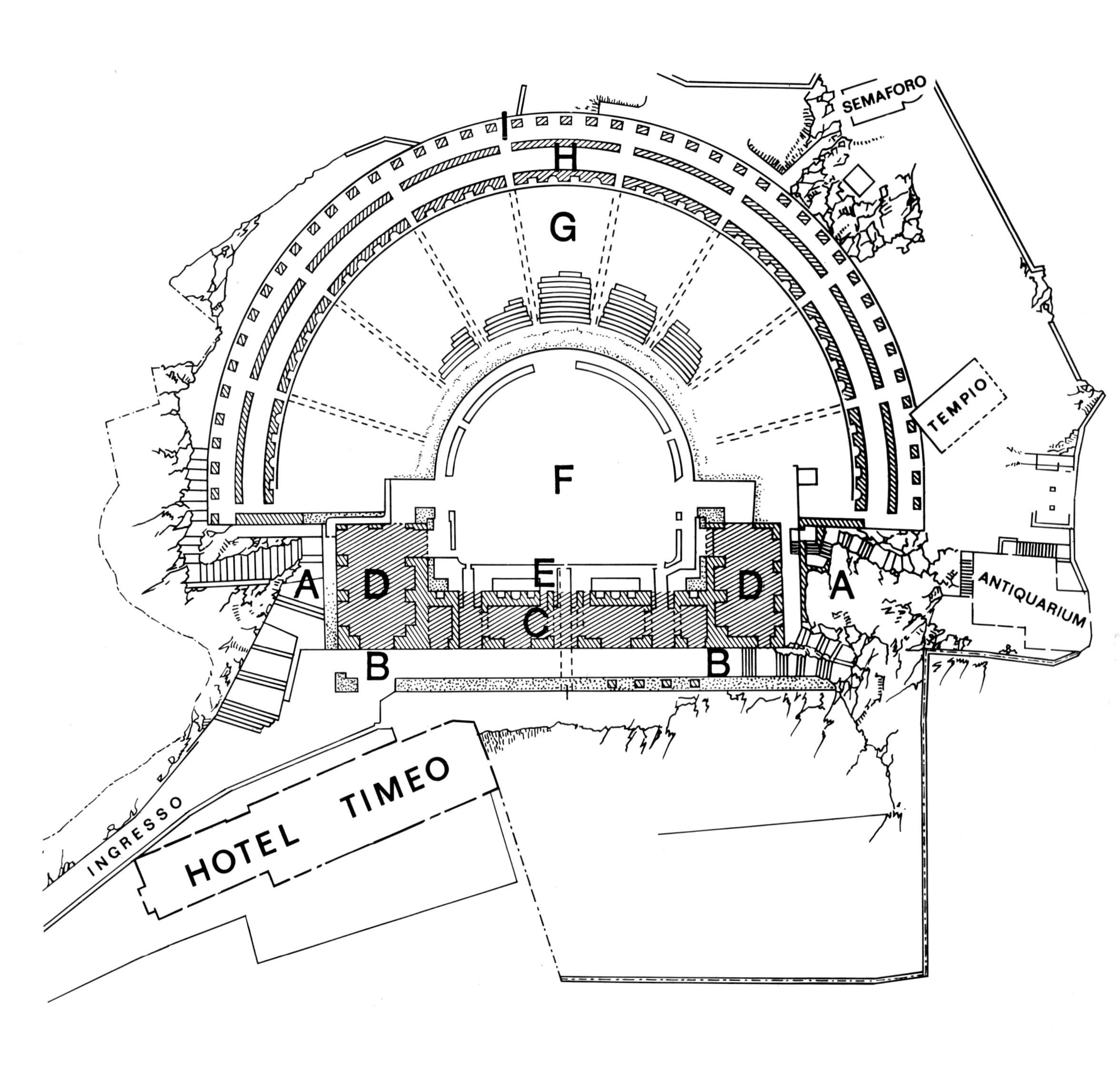

A ENTRANCE TO THE THEATRE

B ENTRANCE TO THE STAGE

C COVERED CORRIDOR TO THE STAGE

D LARGE LATERAL ROOMS

E SCENERY AND STAGE

F ORCHESTRA

G CAVEA OR GRADIN

H 1st. PORTICO (Its vault supported the covered corridor)

I 2nd. PORTICO

The greek-roman theatre

The natural scenery is so attractive that, once transcribed, even the most sublime thoughts would not do credit to the place. It is therefore preferable to leave all sensations complete for those who are lucky enough to visit these places and use the space for a description of the Theatre.

Building of the Hellenic Theatre probably dates back to the third century B.C. when Gerone II was governor. The building was enlarged and modified in Imperial times under Roman domination. It seems that enlargements were made by widening the caveas, and heightening the perimetrical walls, while the original orchestra floor was left untouched. Transport being what it was in those times, it must have taken years just to remove and transport the material for this monumental work.

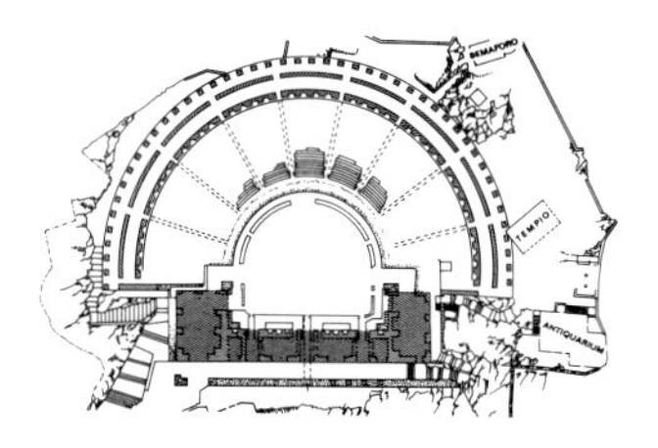

The stage

The most important part of the theatre is the stage which in part has conserved its original form. The stage wall in brick, situated on the east side is 30 meters long by 40. The two large rooms at the sides enclosed the stage. The latter was decorated by two architectural orders, Corinthian in style. The first order, almost against the stage wall, was built of three groups of three granite columns placed in the center and at the two sides. These supported an arched porch which served as a room for the stage. The wall behind the columns had three doors which gave the artists access to the stage, and statues were generally placed in the walls of the niches.

The second architectonic order (logically placed nearer the orchestra) was made up of sixteen lower columns spaced at regular intervals one from the other.

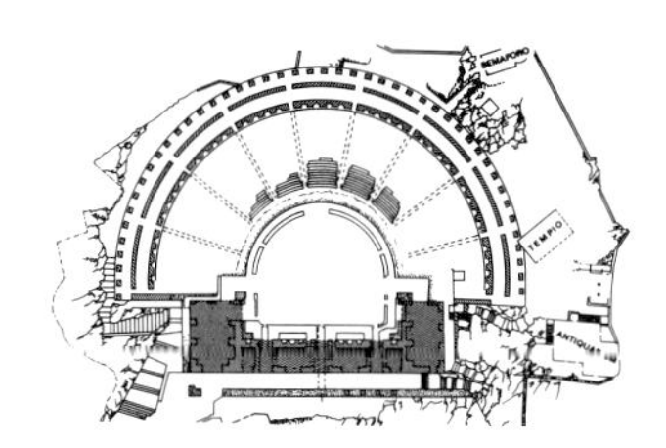

The large lateral rooms

The two large lateral rooms at the sides of the stage shut off the stalls, thus preventing tho publio from paccing through. These served the purpose of the dressing rooms today and as storerooms for stage equipment.

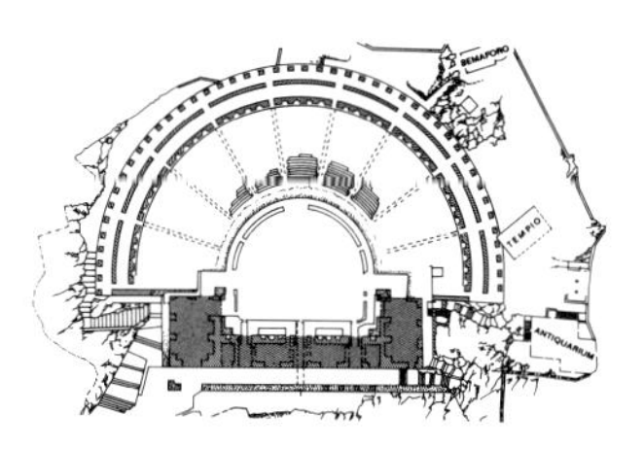

The corridor

The eight little doors led into the covered corridor, which went right round the perimetrical semi-circle of the cavea. The corridor also served to close off the cavea at the two ends (as far as the large rooms). The pavement was supported by the vault of the first portico below.

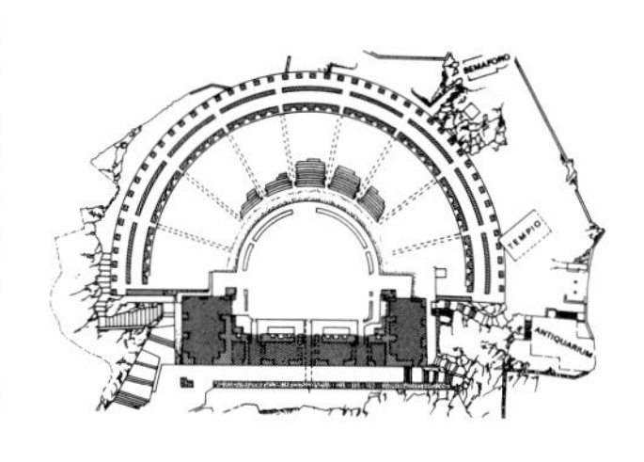

The entrance to the theatre

The public could not enter the theatre from the ground floor. The two big side rooms had a door in the south-facing wall, but these rooms were reserved for the artists, and led only onto the stage through the covered stage corridor and not into the theatre. To the side of the large room (where the passage may still be seen from the north-east corner), there were three entrances which could be reached by means of an external staircase. The so-called Royal or Principal Staircase was made up of three winding flights and at every turn it tapered off. The first flight led to the first seats in the cavea which were reserved for the authorities. The second led into the cavea from the high part, by means of the eight little doors in the covered corridor (which went up to the terrace reserved for the women). The third and last portico led to the plebs' terrace. (There was no communication between the latter and the inside of the theatre).

A very large velarium protected the spectators from the sun's rays or from the rain.

The Theatre had perfect acoustics and held about 5400 spectators.

Over the last few years the Tourist Association has organised performances of a very high standard.

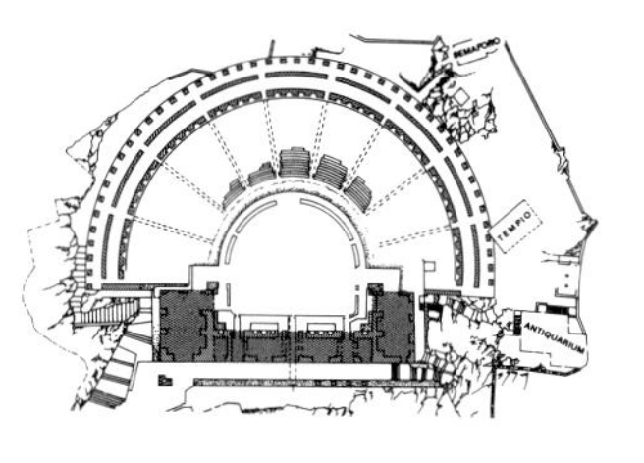

The cavea or stalls

It is built into the rock and has a diameter of 109 meters. (In the whole of Sicily it is second only to the one in Siracusa). It was divided horizontally by five annular passages which separated the arrangement of seats, while eight staircases, made up of thirty steps, divided it vertically into 9 sections.

The flights of steps went up from the stalls and ended high up where eight corresponding doors opened into the covered corridor. In the same end wall of the stalls in the space between one door and another there were niches which held statues representing famous playwrights.

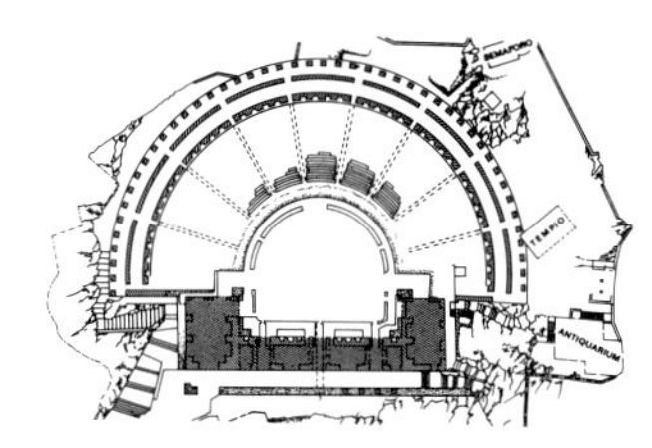

The orchestra

This was reserved for the players and chorus. It was enlarged (it measures 35 meters) and surrounded by a protective platform, thus eliminating the stage.

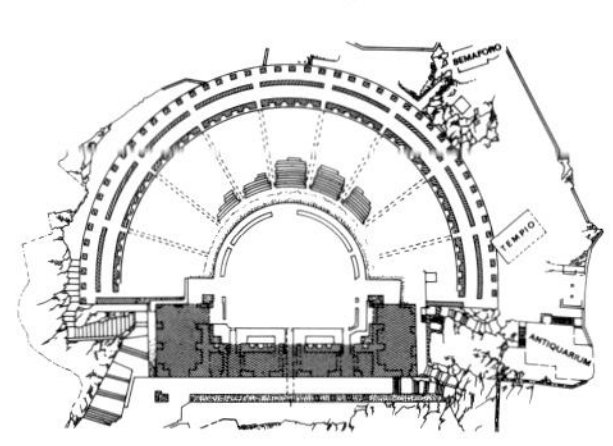

The porticos

There were two porticos, one alongside the other. The inner one was lower than the external one. The first and lower one (leaving from the center of the theatre), supported the covered corridor on its vault, and its ceiling in its turn supported a terrace, on which there were wooden seats. These seats were reserved for the women. The other external, higher portico also supported a terrace (higher than the one already described) without seats, reserved for the plebs.

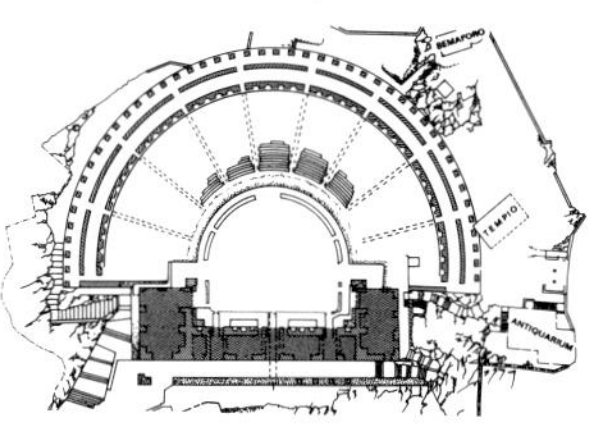

The antiquarium

Next to the theatre is the museum. It houses various archeological finds from the Theatre and ancient Taormina. There are some extremely interesting marble relics and particularly noteworthy are the fragments of sarcophagi, statues of young men's torsos, a woman's head, cippi, inscribed tombstones, and a two-footed centauress as well as other fragments of clay sculptures. There are also bronzes, fragments of mosaic floors, earthenware vascular paintings and various handmade articles.

text edited by ROBERTO ALDROVANDI

The end part of the covered corridor which crowned the entire perimetre of the *cavea*, the tiered rows of seats. Foreground: the flooring mosaic of the small Greek temple, two different stair types of which exist underneath the structures dating to Roman times. A small Antiquarium has been set up near the temple for the display of artifacts from the amphitheatre and other monuments of Taormina. Of special interest are the epigraphs and inscriptions which range in date from 150 B.C. to the period of the Roman Empire. Several tablets refer to city officials and administration: the *Tamiai*, public tax officials, the *Hieromnamones*, guardians of sacred objects, and the *Agoranomoi*, the police of Tauromenion. There is a list in Greek etched on marble tablets of the *strategoi* and *gymnasiarchs*, and two epigraphs refer to the cults of Demeter and Kore and of Isis and Serapis. Other items of major interest include an ornate sarcophagus with sculpted Bacchus scene and a headless torso of Apollo dating to the Hellenistic period.

According to the inscriptions on several tiers of the *cavea*, the survivors of Naxos who founded Tauromenion with the help of Andromach were soon prosperous enough to erect an amphitheatre in the third century B.C. The main traces of the original Hellenic structure are to be found in the Corinthian remains of the stage and the stone blocks of the *cavea* which have been recovered and reset as the seating tiers. In *ca*. the second century A.D. during the Roman Empire, the amphitheatre was enlarged and almost completely rebuilt. The remains of the stage with their many detailed particulars are the best-preserved examples dating from this time. The columns which actually adorn the back stage wall were put there during restoration in the last century and were not part of the original stage area. The Romans eliminated the proscenium to accommodate gladiatorial combat and installed large troughs in the orchestra so as to stage *naumachie*, or sea battles. Hence the original Greek theatre space assumed the form of the classic Roman amphitheatre.

Facing page: View of the superb panorama as seen from the theatre's *cavea*, including Aetna and the elegant San Domenico Hotel.

Below: Columns and Corinthian capitals together with decorative fragments from various epochs which make the theatre an open-air «antiquarium».

View of the porticoes which ringed the theatre. The inner is lower than the outer one and (starting from the theatre's centre) supported the covered corridor, the roof of which in turn bore up a terrace that accommodated the wooden seats reserved for women. The outer, higher portico also supported a terrace, which was higher than the other and without seats, as it was reserved for the plebians.
There were large rooms at either end of the stage called *parascenia* or parascenes, i.e. they closed off the pit to the entering public which was channelled into the *cavea* by a threeflight stairway at one end of the stage. These parascenes were used to store equipment, scenery and acted as dressing rooms for the performers.

THE ODEON THEATRE - Dating to the Roman Empire, it was erected on the ancient foundations of a Greek temple and unearthed in the modern era in 1893. Apart from musical and theatrical performances, the Odeon was also the scene of official public gatherings. The *cavea* was composed of 16 rising tiers divided into five semi-circular wedges. The stage area utilized the longest side of the earlier Greek temple, the colonnade of which was ideally suited to the new surroundings.

NAUMACHIA (Sea Battle) - It is one of the most imposing of all Roman structures in Sicily and, after the Theatre, the most monumental building of Taormina's antiquities. Grandiose in design, it is 122 m (375 ft) long and was probably used as a gymnasium for athletic practice and contests by naked practitioners of the physical arts. The name *naumachia* was improperly attributed to it because of the large pool used by the athletes after their exercises.

CASA
INCEGNERE

A fine view of the centre of Taormina seen from the square before the small shrine of the Madonna della Rocca. The image eloquently expresses the breathtaking position of the city – suspended between rock and sea, studded by the monuments of the past and the modern tourist «cathedrals» of the present. The discerning visitor, here surrounded by so vibrant a display of nature and in direct contact with the ancient Greek, Roman, Islamic and Norman worlds, cannot but feel that which words alone would be inadequate to express yet which will remain indelibly etched in mind and heart.

(Bottom of page) View of CASA FLORESTA dating from the 1400-1500s. It is an excellent example of that particular artistic expression in architectural forms blending elements of Gothic, Catalan, Arabic and Norman in a unique harmonious whole so typical of Taormina's cultural heritage. (Adjacent) Another example of a private habitation from the same feudal period with its fine «chiaramontana» mullioned window.
The parapet merlons of the Badia Vecchia stand out starkly against the sunset and fire of Aetna in eruption.

The necessarily brief photographic synopsis presented on this page is an attempt, albeit with rather tentative results, to portray the majestic beauty of Taormina. Its milleniums of history, the magnificent and often unique monuments from the ancient and medieval epochs, its extraordinary climate and the breath-taking splendour of its panoramas make Taormina the indisputable «queen» of the Mediterranean. With its aristocratic grace and hospitality, it continues to celebrate and unfold its magic spell, sharing with the unhurried and contemplative visitor the nectar of its very essence.

A panoramic view of the north coast near Taormina featuring LETOIANNI, a growing tourist and bathing locale, with its magnificent shore line extending from the Baia delle Sirene (Sirens' Bay) to Capo Sant'Alessio (Cape St Alexis). Situated on the sloping hills and immersed in the luxuriant effusion of nature, its fine hotels pensions, famous restaurants and well-outfitted, comfortable camp grounds play host to increasing numbers of visitors every year.

PALAZZO CORVAIA - Erected on the site of the ancient Roman Forum in the 15th century, it features an incorporated Arab tower and earlier 14th-century building. Originally the property of the Zumbos of Taormina, it was next owned by the Rossos d'Altavilla and then by the Corvaias, all of whom were local nobles. Site of the first Sicilian Parliament, called into being to elect Federico di Luna King of Sicily in 1410, this Quattrocento palazzo is yet again another example of the area's architectural eclecticism, featuring the solid Gothic wedded to elements of the Catalan, Arabic-norman and «chiaramontana». These include such details as horseshoe-arch mullioned windows, ornate battlements with side lobes, Catalan-inspired portals with drop arches, and the external access stairways of polychromed pumice and lava inlays forming singularly beautiful lace-work patterns along the decorative bands adorning the façades. Despite this myriad of stylistic devices, the whole is harmoniously blended by the strong Spanish influence. ESTO.MICHII. LOCU. REFUGII., my place of refuge, is inscribed under one of the mullioned windows of the inner courtyard in tribute to the solace the palazzo once afforded its noble owner.

Latin inscriptions in Gothic script—moral maxims regarding justice, prudence, fortitude and temperance—can be seen on the cornice below the four mullioned windows adorning the façade. (Preceding page: The portal and three-light mullioned window on the south façade of Palazzo Corvaia).

THE DUOMO (San Nicola, St Nicholas) - Initially erected in the 13th century over the remains of a pre-existing church, the Duomo was rebuilt in the 15th and 16th centuries and refurbished in the 1700s. The angular and austere forms of the exterior recall the Norman cathedrals. The façade features a portal (1636), flanked by two pointed-arch windows, and, above, a delicately ornate, small rose window from the 1500s. The interior is laid out in three naves separated by two rows of marble columns which support pointed arches. The central nave and transept lie under a wooden ceiling the trusses of which are supported by corbels with Arab-inspired inlay work. An impressive collection of fine gold pieces from different epochs is on display in the sacresty.

Two of the works of art in the Duomo: (Above) The Visitation, with St Joseph and Zachariah, by Antonio Giuffrè, *ca*. 1457.

(Adjacent) Detail of the triptych «Madonna and Child» showing four saints and pietà, by Antonello de Saliba, 1504.

GERONIMO

D O M

TAXI

PALAZZO DEI DUCHI DI SANTO STEFANO (Palazzo of the Dukes of St Stephen) - Still enclosed by the old city walls at the end of a medieval street before Porta Catania is Palazzo S. Stefano. First erected towards the end of the 1300s but not finished until the early 1400s, it was initially the property of the Santo Stefanos, dukes of Spain. After being restored to its original splendour following the damage brought by the Second World War, the palazzo is another fine example of that unique Sicilian architecture of the time, blending the Gothic, Catalan, Arab-norman and «chiaramontana» traditions. A large tower-like structure of square plan, the interior consists of three floors with large rooms throughout. Lighting is provided by a series of pointed mullioned windows (those in correspondence with the main floor are of exceptional artistry). The large room on the ground floor features a groin or cross vault, the arches of which are supported by a central column.

(Above) East façade showing the entrance portal beneath the crest of the Dukes of St Stephen and the outer stairs.

(Adjacent) Polychromed mesh band in limestone and ▸ lava above one of the main-storey mullioned windows.

Facing page: Night view of the Piazza Municipio (City Hall Square) with the Duomo and the Baroque fountain (1635).

◂ The two white marble portals on the sides of the basilica. The one on the left dates from the 1500s and the other, delicately adorned with vine-tendril motif, is from the 1400s.

PIAZZA IX APRILE (9th of April Piazza) - It interrupts Corso Umberto I° (Avenue Umberto I), the city's main thoroughfare which runs from Porta Messina to Porta Catania and crosses the square. The tables of the caffés bordering the square make the piazza the ideal place for a pleasant stop, whether to have coffee early in the morning, an aperitif before meals, or some fine Sicilian ice-cream on a cool summer's eve.
Visitors will find a cosmopolitan world here in this square – a Babel of languages and nationalities, northern Europeans, Africans, Americans, and Near and Far Easterners. It is, in short, Taormina's hospitable, public reception hall.
There is another superb panorama from the railed promenade on one side of the square – the Graeco-roman theatre atop its green hill, the splendid Bay of Giardini protected by the small, Schisò peninsula and towering Aetna to the south, firey red in the evening.

◄ (Facing page) View of the south façade and the palazzo's three storeys.

Several monuments from different epochs ring the piazza. The oldest is the Torre dell'Orologio (Clock Tower), also called the «Porta di Mezzo» (Mid-Gate), which was erected *ca*. 13th century on graeco-roman foundations. (Right) The former church of St Augustine, built in 1448, with its fine pointed-arch portal beneath a small rose window, low Gothic-arch bell tower, single interior nave and double-slope roof, is today the seat of the communal library.

At the top of a double stairway is the church of San Giuseppe (St Joseph). Erected at the end of the 17th century in an unadorned Baroque style, it features a façade with fluted weathering and cusped bell tower (standing free of the church). The interior has fine 18th-century stucco work.

(Above) The coat of arms of Taormina: A female centaur, with crown, holding a globe in its left hand.

A picturesque stairway ascends towards the slopes of Mt Tauro from one of the caffés in the Piazza IX Aprile. The «eagle's nest» of Castel Taormina dominates the view.

Mocambo
Mocambo
Mocambo
Mocambo

VELLODORO
ETTORE
CONI CON PANNA

(Facing page, above) The Santuario della Madonna della Rocca (The Shrine of the Madonna of the Rock). A magnificent and breath-taking view of the sheer drop and the limestone rocks studded with prickly pear trees below awaits the visitor from the terrace in front of the Shrine. The feast of the Madonna is celebrated in September.

(Below) Snow-capped Aetna seen from the slopes of Castel Taormina which are covered by the prickly pear trees.

CASTEL MOLA - Almost inaccessible 500 metres atop its imposing limestone rocks, it is the true «belvedere» of the area comprising Taormina. After a swim in the limpid Ionian, or a sight-filled excursion to Aetna, nothing is more gratifying than a relaxing stroll through the medieval lanes of the town and a refreshing stop on the terrace of the San Giorgio caffé. The drinks are cool, the view spectacular, and the proprietor, Mr Blandano, is an affable gentleman and ready conversationalist, always willing to speak of the illustrious guests he has played host to in his establishment. He has even collected their autographs in a series of volumes he keeps in the caffé. Aristocrats from all over Europe, statesmen from the four corners of the world, princes and Oriental monarchs, writers and artists, magnates of industry and of international finance, and everyone who has fallen in love with this unique area. All who have ventured to this spot and crossed the caffé's threshold have found their host's amiable courtesy and charm always ready to greet them at any hour of the day, and even far into the night.

In ancient times, Castel Mola was settled by the Siculans as evidenced by a necropolis which was unearthed at Cocolonazzo, a site at the foot of the rock upon which the town stands. Many references speak of it as the ancient Mylai, an impregnable fortified outpost which successfully repulsed invaders from the inland areas. In 392 B.C. it was destroyed by Dionysius of Syracuse during the war against the Carthaginians. Rebuilt in 350 B.C., it was used as a strong hold by rebels in the Slave Wars, and was again razed to the ground by the Moslem forces in 902 A.D.

Panorama of Castel Mola from the battlements of Castel Taormina.

A view of the narrow streets and bell tower of the Duomo.

The small church of San Giorgio (St George) rising above the sun-drenched picturesque lanes of Mola.
The ruins of the 16th-century castle situated on the town's highest point in the public gardens.

The main square of **CASTEL MOLA**, on the road from Taormina, and a beautiful belvedere which looks onto the Ionian sea, on the Sicilian and Calabrian coast. The attractive waterfront has been one of the defensive bulwark of the ancient town for many centuries.

Near the group of houses, there are remains of a necropolis (10th-7th century) and at the highest point of the rock, there are the remains of a (15th century) castle, built on long-standing medieval fortifications.

The cable-car service which connects Taormina to the lidos of Mazzarò and Isola Bella in a few minutes.

A guide through the pleasures of Taormina would be incomplete if Sicilian cuisine were left unmentioned. The finely set tables offer a superb variety of the island's culinary art and traditions. For on the one hand we have the genuine fresh produce of the farms and orchards, the variety of rich meats from grazing livestock, the generous offerings of the abundant sea, all of which endow even the most simple foods with a full and extraordinary flavour; and on the other the intoxicating wealth of specialties which once graced the tables of the Norman, Islamic, Swabian, Anjous and Bourbon courts. What more can be said of the vegetables from Gela, which ripen naturally in January without the need of greenhouses, the herds which graze on the upland pastures of the Madonie and Nebrodi, the fish, lobsters, shrimp, tuna and mythical sword-fish which daily find their way from the sea of Sicily to the table? Indeed, this too is Sicily!

THE GORGES OF ALCANTARA

The valley at the bottom of Etna, is crossed by the Alcantara river on the north-eastern side. This name came from Arab and means «the bridge», referring to the bridge which stood above the consular road between Catania and Messina. It is situated at the bottom of «Pizzo Inferno», it crosses Randazzo and Mojo Alcantara and winds up the slopes of Etna, among the lava flows which mark the centuries, forming a provacative small lake in their tortuous gorges. Then, it reaches Francavilla, and here it winds to another lava flow which sprang up from the subthermal cone of Mojo. This flow formed the preseet peninsula of Schisò, where in 735 B.C. the Greeks landed and built Naxos, their first settlement in Sicily. In the narrow gorge, which recalls Dante's Hell, the continuous erosion of wind and water has formed jagged basalt rocks over the centuries. The clear waters form small pools and lakes with glistening reflections, thanks to the suns' rays which aren't able to reach every corner of the narrow gorges.

The river, then, reaches a sweet-smelling valley, covered with olanders, rhododendrous and orange trees, and the contrast between the neighbouring landscape makes the unique sight of these places quite unforgetable.

The Sicilian cart, fruit of artistic workmanship, has recen origins. Only in the second half of the 19th century did the car begin to contribute to picturesque scenes and figurative engravings. The use of the decorated cart developed mainly around Catania and Palermo, and it seems that the latter has the primacy of the more artistically «serious» paintings. They were decorated with imaginary characters and sum up the more vivacious and picturesque characteristics of Sicilian spirit.

A folkloristic group dressed with the traditional regiona costumes. The rich clothes show the lace tecnique which has centuries-old tradition, dating back to the Arab-Norma domination.

FOLKLORE

The work of the marionettes. The theatre of Marionettes, linked to the chivalrous Arab-Norman traditions and with the French paladines, has recent origins, even if performances of Marionette had already taken places in ancient Syracuse. The legends of Damsels and knights, the idealized character of Roger who slaughters the Muslims, the knights of the Round Table, the Carolingians and King Arthur, are the characters and the performers of the 1000 stories, told by the «Pupara» (puppeteers). But even if before the 19th century, the ballad-singers with their painted stage-scenary retold the «great feats» of the French paladines and Knight's legends of every age.

But these aspects of the Sicilian folklore, are only a small part of the popular traditions so rich in elements of island folklore. It is enough to think about the beautiful parties, the thriumphant wagons of the patron saints, the figurative procession, the historical rides, which are all shows linked to religious ends to splendid humanity, to generous and joyful impulses and sometimes, to a tragic sentimentalism belonging to Sicilian nature. The great folklorist well-known in Europe, Giuseppe Pitrè from Palermo, writes in his book «Biblioteca delle tradizioni popolari» (a collection of popular traditions) that «in Italy there are not other regions like Sicily, where so many and different way of living exist...».

«The innumerable dominations of the island left deep marks in the way of dressing, in the heart, the imagination as well as in the faces and surname of every Sicilian». In Sicily the past is not dead; it lives with us and inside us, it is with us in our weeding bed, from the cradle to the coffin, in parties and plays, in spectacles, and in churches in the streets and in the fields, it lives and speaks everywhere. History is not only what is written in textbooks, but it is also what is shown by the popular traditions and beliefs».

AETNA - THE LARGEST VOLCANO IN EUROPE.

The mythological forge of Vulcan, situated in the Province of Catania, rises above the valleys bounded on the north by the Alcantara river and on the south by the Simeto river and the sea. Encompassing a total perimeter of more than 200 km and an area of about 1600 km², Aetna originated from undersea eruptions which gradually formed the cyclopian mountain and shaped the surrounding terrain and coastline. The continuous volcanic eruptions and lava flows cause dramatic fluctuations in its height, i.e. from 3313 metres in the mid-1800s to 3274 metres at the beginning of this century, while in 1960 it was 3296 m and in 1966 it fell to 3226 m. There have been 137 eruptions in recorded history, one of the most tremendous of which was the one in 396 B.C. when the lava flow reached the sea. There have also been a series of catastrophic eruptions, beginning with that in 1329 and in 1381, in which the molten rock reached the city of Catania. Next was the eruption of 1669 which, preceded by days of disastrous earthquakes, gave rise to the Monti Rossi (Red Mountains) near the town of Nicolosi, engulfed several villages and buried districts of Catania before reaching the sea. Other ruinous eruptions were recorded in 1917, when the lava flow reached a height of 850 metres, covering the surrounding area with over three million cubic metres of ash and firey rock; in 1923, in 1928, causing the destruction of Mascali; and in 1950-1951, when the lava flowed for more than a year, emptying more than eight-hundred and fifty million cubic metres of detritus in the area. Today most of these areas have been replanted with chestnuts, birches, pines and larches. And, although above 2000 metres, the vegetation is scarce because of the lava flows, the area at the foot of the mountain is a panoply of nature—pistachio trees, citrus groves, orchards and vineyards which produce excellent, quality wines.

Photos: Several views of the volcano.

GIARDINI - Several facets of the town of Giardini. It has developed into an increasingly important tourist site by virtue of its location at the mouth of the Alcantara river, its fine beaches, and the comforts afforded by its facilities and management resources. (Above) The fishing fleet port and, in the background, the mountains with Taormina and Castel Mola. (Adjacent) The hotel area dominated by the imposing Mt Aetna. (Facing page) View of the town from the Graeco-roman theatre of Taormina.

SALVATORE

NAXOS. In 734 B.C., Theocles, at the head of a group of colonists from Calchis, landed on the Schisò peninsula and founded not far away the first Greek colony in Sicily. The name probably derives from some of these settlers who came from Naxos, the Aegean island of the same name in the Cyclades, and wanted to honour their home. It is presumed that the years following its founding were prosperous as colonists were later sent forth to found Callipolis.

In 498 the settlement is occupied by Hypocrates of Gela, and in 476 B.C., during the reign of Geron I, its inhabitants are deported to Leontinoi. Replaced by Doric colonists, they are later able to return to Naxos.
Naxos was the ally of Athens in the wars between Syracuse and Athens in 433 and 415. Dionysius conquered the town in 403 B.C., through the betrayal of Procles, and razed it to the ground. Thc pcople were enslaved or exiled to Miles, the city founded by Andromach on Mt Tauro — modern Taormina.

Photos: Several images of the Archaeological Park of ancient Naxos.

CASTLE OF ST. ALEXIS - FORZA D'AGRÒ - Placed on a peak above the Ionian sea, on the rocky mountains of Cape St. Alexis, the majestic and embittered castle of St. Alexis, which was called by the Greeks «Argennon akron» (silver cape). The circular building of the castle; crowned by a cylindrical tower rises on a hill near the Catania-Messina road. The rocky spur points down to the sea while a polygonal armoured fortification points up to the sky. The castle once belonged to the noble family of Marquis Mauro, then it was partially rebuilt by the English at the beginning of the 19th century. From the pass at Cape St. Alexis, one can climb up along winding roads which reach a small town Forza d'Agrò, which faces the Ionian sea at 429 m. above sea level. From the outskirts of the town a small group of houses, a beautiful sight reveals the Sicilian coast, as far as the strait and to Calabria. The pictoresque position of Forza d'Agrò, and its unchanged medieval style of Norman origins are a suggestive attraction for the less superficial tourist.

◂ The splendid Gothic-catalan portal at the top of the stairs of piazza SS. Trinità (Holy Trinity Piazza).

By turning off the Statale (highway) 114 at the forbidding Sant'Alessio castle, which dominates the area from atop the Cape of the same name, one reaches the picturesque town of Forza D'Agrò, after a steep and tortuous ascent along the winding road. It is one of the most splendid sights that Sicily has to offer. One's gaze sweeps out from a height of 429 metres over the Strait of Messina, the Calabrian coast and the indented shoreline of eastern Sicily. The town's superb location and intact medieval Norman character make Forza d'Agrò an important stop on any tourist itinerary.

(Right) The bell tower and church of the Triade, which is crowned by the portal leading to the square in front.

(Below) Panorama of the town from the medieval castle. In the centre, the Baroque church of the Matrice (1700s).

Tourist Board (E.P.T.) Concession in Catania